THE WEDDING RING AND ADORNMENT:

An Analysis and Appeal

Clyde Morgan

Amazing Facts, Inc.
P.O. Box 1058
Roseville, CA 95678-8058
www.amazingfacts.org

Edited by Anthony Lester
Cover Design by Haley Trimmer
Layout by Greg Solie - Altamont Graphics
Final Copy Proof by Tarah Solie

ISBN 1-58019-149-5

THE WEDDING RING AND ADORNMENT:
An Analysis and Appeal

Contents

Preface

The controversy surrounding the wedding ring has plagued the Christian church since its inception. As the church moved through history, her different groups broke away from the standard convention that the wedding ring was to be avoided because of its pagan origins. Many denominations no longer forbade its use, and indeed incorporated it into the wedding ceremony itself. However, this issue has not become passé in the larger church arena, as many groups ignore this general trend and still admonish its followers to avoid the wearing of jewelry. One such church is the Seventh-day Adventist Church. This Sabbath-keeping, Christian denomination has recently been forced to address this issue because some members want to ease the doctrine of wedding rings and other adornment. In response to this controversy, Clyde Morgan writes the following argument for keeping the long-held Adventist position that any form of adornment, including the wedding ring, is a reproach on God's moral standards.

—Amazing Facts

Introduction

*"Lifestyle religion, the absorbing concern for
appearance, is not the heart of the Gospel."*
—Alan Williams[1]

Mr. Williams is correct. The matter of concern for appearance, including the wedding
ring, is certainly not the heart of the gospel. I
affirm that the core of the gospel is that Jesus
died to save sinners, and that all who recognize
their sinfulness and flee to the Savior for forgive-
ness and salvation may receive it freely, "not of
works, lest anyone should boast."[2] My own heart
and life have been gripped by a loving Savior
who accepted me where I was and has continued
to love and patiently guide me toward His eter-
nal kingdom. I praise Him!

The gospel also teaches that those who have
received Christ, and have been captured by His
love, will more and more desire to obey and to
please Him in all things. And while there is a pri-
ority of matters facing the Christian, the true,
persevering disciple will never turn back and say
to the Lord: "This thing You have asked of me is
too small a matter. I will not give it any heed."
Instead, it is in the heart of the true Christian to
eagerly "follow the Lamb wherever He goes."[3]

It is with this spirit that I wish to approach
the matter of adornment and the wedding ring.

Without an understanding of how the use of jewelry and the wedding ring developed, it would be difficult to understand the significance of decisions we now make or their implications for the future. Therefore I begin with a survey of the subject and will then present reasons why I believe the Seventh-day Adventist Church should reject and abandon the practice, and why I believe each member should place his or her influence on this side. It is my prayer that God's last-day people will "hear what the Spirit says to the churches."[4]

---

[1]"American Epitaph for a Third-World Church," Letters to the Editor, *Adventist Today*, May-June, 1996, p. 6.

[2] *Ephesians 2:9*. Unless otherwise noted, all Scripture quotations are from the *New King James Version* of the Bible.

[3] *Revelation 14:4*.

[4] *Revelation 3:22*.

Survey of the Development and Use of the Wedding Ring

"We have nothing to fear for the future, except as we shall forget the way the Lord has led us, and His teaching in our past history."
—Ellen White[1]

Though its beginnings are murky and not well-recorded, the wedding ring appears to have arisen in the ancient Near East before being picked up by the Greeks and passed on to the Romans. Cardinal Newman says it came into the Christian church from pagan Rome,[2] but apparently it was not adopted until some centuries after Christ.[3] So, obviously, it is not specifically addressed in Scripture. However, the practices of wearing other finger rings and various other forms of jewelry were in existence in Bible times and are addressed in Scripture. Signet rings were used by kings,[4] and early Mesopotamian peoples, including Abraham's family,[5] used jewelry. The Egyptians used jewelry and, following Moses' instructions, the Israelites took jewelry and clothing from the Egyptians upon their departure from Egypt, apparently as payment for their years of slave labor.[6] Later, much of this gold and silver was used in the construction of the wilderness tabernacle.[7]

Many of the references to adornment and jewelry in Scripture are figurative, taking the form of allegory,[8] parable,[9] or simile.[10] Sometimes the figurative reference reflects favorably upon such adornment[11] and sometimes negatively, associating it with immorality and godlessness.[12] In the experience of God's people, the use of jewelry is typically associated with compromise and the adoption of idolatry or other practices of the pagan nations around them. On the other hand, periods of reform and drawing near to God were typically associated with the abandonment of such practices, including wearing jewelry.[13] The Bible records at least two instances in Old Testament times when the Israelites were specifically called upon to remove their jewelry and ornamentation:

Then God said to Jacob, 'Arise, go up to Bethel and dwell there; and make an altar there to God, who appeared to you when you fled from the face of Esau your brother. And Jacob said to his household and to all who were with him, 'Put away the foreign gods that are among you, purify yourselves, and change your garments ... so they gave Jacob all the foreign gods which were in their hands, and the earrings which were in their ears; and Jacob hid them under the terebinth tree which was by Shechem.[14]

For the LORD had said to Moses, 'Say to the children of Israel, You are a stiff necked people. I could come up into your midst in one moment and consume you. Now therefore, take off your ornaments, that I may know what to do to you.' So the children of Israel stripped themselves of their ornaments by Mount Horeb.[15]

The New Testament is even clearer on the subject, with both Paul and Peter expressing the divine will that believers should avoid jewelry and the latest fashions.

In like manner also, that the women adorn themselves in modest apparel, with propriety and moderation, not with braided hair or gold or pearls or costly clothing, but, which is proper for women professing godliness, with good works.[16]

Do not let your adornment be merely outward—arranging the hair, wearing gold, or putting on fine apparel—rather let it be the hidden person of the heart, with the incorruptible beauty of a gentle and quiet spirit, which is very precious in the sight of God. For in this manner, in former times, the holy women who trusted in God also adorned themselves ...[17]

Ellen White picked up the refrain centuries later when she quoted the above passage from the apostle Peter and then wrote:

"All that we urge is compliance with the injunctions of God's word. Are we Bible readers and followers of Bible teachings? Will we obey God, or conform to the customs of the world? Will we serve God or mammon? Can we expect to enjoy peace of mind and the approval of God while walking directly contrary to the teachings of His word?

"The apostle Paul exhorts Christians not to be conformed to the world, but to be transformed by the renewing of the mind, 'that ye may prove what is that good, and acceptable, and perfect, will of God.' But many who profess to be children of God feel no scruples against conforming to the customs of the world in the wearing of gold and pearls and costly array. Those who are too conscientious to wear these things are regarded as narrow-minded, superstitious, and even fanatical. But it is God who condescends to give us these instructions; they are the declarations of Infinite Wisdom, and those who disregard them do so at their own peril and loss."[18]

A few pages later, still relating to the same Bible passage, she wrote:

> "Obedience to fashion is pervading our Seventh-day Adventist churches and is doing more than any other power to separate our people from God. ... There is a terrible sin upon us as a people, that we have permitted our church members to dress in a manner inconsistent with their faith. We must arise at once and close the door against the allurements of fashion. Unless we do this, our churches will become demoralized."[19]

Following the Protestant Reformation, Catholic churches and some Protestant churches such as the Anglicans[20] and Lutherans continued the practice of the wearing of jewelry, including the wedding ring. However, other churches arising out of the Reformation abandoned jewelry, including the wedding ring. These included churches such as the Presbyterians[21] and Baptists.[22] Subsequent revivals brought further reform by groups such as the Puritans[23] and Methodists.[24]

Many of the people involved in the Great Second Advent Awakening of the 1830s and 1840s came from such churches. At that time, these churches did not permit the use of jewelry, including the wedding ring, on the basis of their understanding of the Biblical call for simplicity of dress and the leaving off of outward adornment.[25] Adventists understood it the same way and carried these principles into their new associations and later into the Seventh-day Adventist Church.

The churches, including our own, that believed God had asked them to leave off jewelry included the wedding ring in this category. No distinction was made between the wedding ring and other jewelry. This was a later, more modern innovation.

At about the same time that the Seventh-day Adventist Church was officially forming (1863), the prohibition against the wedding ring was beginning to break down in the very churches from which many of the Adventists had come. It was breaking down in the Baptist churches as early as 1857 and had broken down in the Methodist and Presbyterian churches by 1872 and 1873, respectively. All of these churches, without exception, soon went on to adopt jewelry in all of its various forms.

Adventists saw this and lamented the fact. In 1869 Daniel T. Bourdeau wrote:

> "Not many years since it was considered a sin by Baptists, Methodists, and other denominations, to wear gold; and I well remember when the Baptists, to whom I belonged, and who used to enjoy more of the spirit of God than they now do, made it a rule to take up a labor, in love, with those members who put on gold. But for

quite a number of years the different denominations have undergone a great change on this point, and have almost universally adopted the practice of wearing gold and other vain ornaments."[26]

In an article in the *Second Advent Review and Sabbath Herald* in 1880, Ellen White wrote what appears to be her first specific statement regarding the wedding ring, though she had often written regarding the underlying Biblical principles:

"Have not our sisters sufficient zeal and moral courage to place themselves without excuse upon the Bible platform? The inspired apostle has given most explicit directions on this point: *'Whose adorning, let it not be that outward adorning of plaiting the hair, and of wearing of gold, or of putting on of apparel; but let it be the hidden man of the heart, in that which is not corruptible, even the ornament of a meek and quiet spirit, which is in the sight of God of great price.'* Here the Lord, through His apostle, speaks expressly against the wearing of gold. Let those who have had experience see to it that they do not lead others astray on this point by their example. That ring encircling your finger may be very plain, but it is useless, and the wearing of it has a wrong influence upon others."[27]

Two years later, in 1882, she wrote an article that appeared in the same magazine entitled "Where Are We Drifting?" In it she related this incident, which took place at one of the Adventist institutions in Battle Creek, Michigan:

"Mrs. D., a lady occupying a position in the institution, was visiting at Sister _____'s room one day, when the latter took out of her trunk a gold necklace and chain, and said she wished to dispose of this jewelry and put the proceeds into the Lord's treasury. Said the other, 'Why do you sell it? I would wear it if it was mine.' 'Why,' … replied Sister _____, 'when I received the truth, I was taught that all these things must be laid aside. Surely they are contrary to the teachings of God's word.' And she cited her hearer to the words of the apostles, Paul and Peter, upon this point … [quotes *1 Timothy 2:9-10* and *1 Peter 3:3-4*].

"In answer, the lady displayed a gold ring on her finger, given her by an unbeliever, and said she thought it no harm to wear such ornaments. 'We are not so particular,' said she, 'as formerly. Our people have been over-scrupulous in their opinions upon the subject of dress. The ladies of this institution wear gold watches and gold chains, and dress like other people.

It is not good policy to be singular in our dress; for we cannot exert so much influence.'

"We inquire, Is this in accordance with the teachings of Christ? Are we to follow the word of God, or the customs of the world? Our sister decided that it was safest to adhere to the Bible standard. Will Mrs. D. and others who pursue a similar course be pleased to meet the result of their influence, in that day when every man shall receive according to his works?

"God's word is plain. Its teachings cannot be mistaken. Shall we obey it, just as he has given it to us, or shall we seek to find how far we can digress and yet be saved?"[28]

Ten years later, in 1892, while living in Australia and observing the wives of some American missionaries seeking to adopt the wedding ring, she wrote her major statement on the subject. In it she decried the "leavening process which seems to be going on among us, in the conformity to custom and fashion."[29] While making an accommodation for members living in some countries, the clear thrust of the statement is to urge members away from the practice, not toward it.

Over the ensuing decades, the matter of the wedding ring and adornment continued to be agitated, as is evidenced by the articles appearing in denominational publications from time to time. Consistently, however, the denomination took a stand against the practice of the wedding ring, except that it was willing to accommodate members in some countries because of Ellen White's 1892 statement. [30]

In the North American Division, all workers, regardless of where they came from, were asked not to wear a wedding ring. For many years this was done without too much questioning. However, as the staff in North America at the world headquarters and elsewhere became increasingly international, some of these chaffed under "North American rules." There was also more agitation within the North American membership itself. Pressure grew for the church to change its stand on the wedding ring. Finally, in 1972, the church officially addressed the issue.

At a meeting of the General Conference officers in October, they gave counsel on the matter. They first quoted Ellen White's 1892 statement (found in *Testimonies to Ministers*, pp. 180-181 and quoted on page 29 of this book) followed by her 1880 statement (found in *Testimonies for the Church*, Vol. 4, p. 630 and quoted on page 46 of this book). They then gave this counsel:

> On the basis of this inspired counsel and because, in our judgment, the wearing of

the wedding band still "is not regarded as obligatory" or an "imperative" custom in North America, we discourage the use of the wedding band, and counsel our ministers to decline to perform ring ceremonies for church members.

We urge our pastors, evangelists, and Bible Instructors to present fully to candidates for baptism the Bible principles regarding display and adornment; to point out the dangers of clinging to practices, customs and fashions that may be inimical to spiritual development; to press the claims of the gospel upon the conscience of the candidates, encouraging careful self-examination concerning the motives involved in deciding whether to wear the wedding band and to acquaint the candidate with the inspired counsel given by Ellen G. White.

We recognize that some conscientious Seventh-day Adventist Christians believe that conditions in North America have changed greatly since 1892 when Ellen G. White's counsel was given, and that her statement "in countries where the custom is imperative, we have no burden to condemn those who have their marriage ring; let them wear it if they can do so conscientiously" is now applicable to

North America. Therefore, in the absence of explicit instruction in the Bible, in the Spirit of Prophecy writings, or in *The Church Manual,* that would forbid baptism to converts who feel conscientiously that they should wear the wedding band; and in spite of the apparent consensus among Seventh-day Adventists in North America and our historic position here which makes little or no distinction between the wedding band and jewelry that is worn strictly for ornamental purposes; we take the position that a person who on the basis of conscience feels obligated to wear a plain wedding band should not be denied baptism nor forbidden to hold church office.

Inasmuch, however, as the spiritual achievements and ideals of the church are to a great extent a reflection of the spiritual achievements and ideals of its leaders, we appeal to, encourage, and urge our church officers, ministers and their wives, teachers, and other Seventh-day Adventist workers to give strong support through public witness and silent influence, to the counsel in this document and to the standards and principles that have distinguished the remnant church throughout its history, and have kept it separate from the world. We feel concerned that in this final hour of earth's history the church must not lower its standards, blur its identity, or muffle its witness.[31]

At the Annual Council a short time later, these same sentiments were approved through an official vote by the representatives of the world church:

We recommend,

1. That the principles of self-denial, economy, and simplicity should be applied to all areas of life—to our persons, our homes, our churches, and our institutions.

2. That in the area of personal adornment necklaces, earrings, bracelets, rings* (including engagement rings), should not be worn. Articles such as watches, brooches, cuff links, tie clasps, et cetera, should be chosen in harmony with the Christian principles of simplicity, modesty, and economy.

3. That our pastors, evangelists, and Bible instructors present fully to candidates for baptism the Bible principles regarding display and adornment; point out the dangers of clinging to customs and prac-

tices that may be inimical to spiritual development; press the claims of the gospel upon the conscience of the candidates, encouraging careful self-examination concerning the motives involved in decisions that must be made; and acquaint the candidates with the inspired counsel given by Ellen G. White.

As Seventh-day Adventists we believe in the priesthood of all believers. Each soul has direct access to God through Christ, and is accountable to Him for his life and witness. The spiritual condition of the church is basically the sum of the spiritual experience of each individual. In view of this, we urge all our members to commit themselves wholeheartedly to the principles set forth in this recommendation.

Beyond this, and because of the special opportunities that rest with leadership to help the church reach its full potential of spiritual power, we expect our church officers, ministers and their wives, teachers, and other Seventh-day Adventist workers to give strong support to this recommendation through public testimony and example.

In this final hour of earth's history, the church must not lower its standards, blur its identity, or muffle its witness, but must with renewed emphasis give strong support to the standards and principles that have distinguished the remnant church throughout its history and have kept it separate from the world."

* The wording here is that of the recommendation voted by the North American Committee on Administration (NADCA). The recommendation adopted for the entire world field has the qualifying statement "jeweled and other ornamental rings" and omits the parenthetical statement.[32]

In 1974 an article entitled "That Wedding Ring," by an anonymous writer using the pseudonym "Roland Churchman," appeared in *Spectrum*. The author argued several points in favor of permitting the wedding ring in North America. He argued (1) that the church's position against the wedding ring relied "more on the advice of Ellen White than on the teachings of Scripture," (2) "It would spare church members much unnecessary discomfort when explaining the church position to friends of other faiths," (3) "It would spare Adventist women frequent unnecessary embarrassments" such as when a couple stayed in a motel or when the wife is pregnant, and (4) that "it would lead to more effective evangelistic campaigns ... That the church should lose significant numbers of converts by insisting on a requirement of this nature can only be termed a tragedy."[33]

The writer also proposed a strategy for accomplishing the overturning of the church's prohibition on the wedding ring in North America:

> "This new approach would not challenge the authority of Ellen White but would question the interpretations many church leaders have placed on her counsel .... If the church wished, it could make a simple finding of fact that the wearing of the wedding ring in contemporary America is supported by the same firmly rooted social conventions as those that led Mrs. White to tolerate its use abroad."[34]

In other words, the church could simply say that wearing a wedding ring is now considered as imperative in America as in the other countries to which Mrs. White referred in 1892, and therefore it is now okay to wear a wedding ring in North America.

Carl G. Tuland echoed some of the anonymous writer's points in a 1977 *Spectrum* article, but he also added a point. He argued, "This is the crux of the matter, for wearing a wedding band is *not* a question of morals or sin; it is merely one of the customs, which vary with national and social concepts."[35]

As pressures continued to build over the next decade, the North American Division felt compelled to address the issue again. In 1986 at its year-end meetings, it passed the following action:

Voted,

1. To reaffirm the principles regarding personal adornment as outlined in *The Church Manual*, the 1972 Annual Council action, and the General Conference officers' statement of October 2, 1972.

2. To affirm that the wearing of jewelry is unacceptable and is a denial of the principles enunciated in the Bible and Spirit of Prophecy concerning personal adornment.

3. To recognize that, in harmony with the position stated in *The Church Manual* (pp. 145, 146), some church members in the North American Division as in other parts of the world feel that wearing a simple marriage band is a symbol of faithfulness to the marriage vow and to declare that such persons should be fully

accepted in the fellowship and service of the church.

4. To make an immediate appeal to our people for a commitment to simplicity in lifestyle and by pen, voice, and example to halt the rising tide of worldly attitudes and practices that have made their subtle appearance within the church in recent years.[36]

This action was interpreted by many to mean an open door for any member, minister, or church leader in North America to wear a wedding ring with full acceptance. One ordained pastor reported that the Sabbath after the action was announced, six couples in his small church, "who had never worn rings before, showed up wearing them."[37] However, the fact that the action reaffirmed the 1972 statements and didn't materially change anything was lost in the rush to adopt the practice.

Calvin B. Rock, General Conference general vice president, characterized the 1986 NAD action thus:

"While the custom of wearing a wedding ring has become important to an increasing percentage of the American population, it does not carry here the cultural imperatives that Ellen White recognized in older, more traditional societies."[38]

In 1987 one author wrote a curious statement. After quoting part of Ellen White's 1892 statement, he opined:

"She was speaking of the simple unadorned wedding band. A jewel-encrusted wedding band would be as out of place as any other ring, for all ornamental jewelry was outside the pale for every Adventist, as far as she was concerned. But Ellen White did not consider a simple, unadorned wedding band as ornamental jewelry."[39]

In 1988 another church leader wrote, "Those who do not choose to adopt this custom, and who also refuse to condemn those who do, align themselves with the true spirit of the division's position."[40] He did, however, second the idea that the wedding ring is not jewelry.

One Seventh-day Adventist evangelist wrote of the 1986 action:

"The distorted message which reached most of our ministers and our people was simply 'it's alright for us to wear a wedding ring now.' ... The fact is that both the letter and the spirit of the Council's action is being violated and ignored by the majority of pastors and members. The ironic thing is that the pastors who are following the conditions laid down by the action [pressing the claims of the gospel and presenting the Spirit of Prophecy counsel to baptismal candidates] are the ones being accused of disloyalty and rebellion. They are falsely perceived as resisting some carte blanche church approval of the wedding ring which is not the case at all."[41]

Concerning the type of distinction such as the one the earlier writer sought to make between a "jewel-encrusted wedding band" and a "simple unadorned" one, this evangelist went on to say:

"I seriously doubt that a single worker has made an issue over the type or size of the wedding ring. To me it is understandable why they do not follow this part of the policy. Even if it were possible to determine the difference between a simple ring and an "un-simple" one, there is no biblical support for the position that the plain one is acceptable and the other unacceptable. No minister is comfortable in taking arbitrary positions based on church rules rather than God's rules.

"This brings to light the largest problem of all, and explains why most ministers are simply accepting all wedding rings, ignoring the policy requiring them to present Bible and Spirit of Prophecy counsel on the issue. They cannot give Bible evidence for accepting a ring on finger number three and rejecting rings on all other fingers, therefore they ignore the very heart of all the requirements, just as they ignore the size and type of ring being worn. ... What a tragedy indeed that the action which was intended to strengthen our stand against worldly ornamentation has produced exactly the opposite effect."[42]

In 1996, university student Alan Williams disparaged the wedding ring standard, saying: "The issue of the wedding band (and many like it) reveals a haunting preoccupation with the status quo. A church focused on preserving 1950s values cannot meet the needs or appeal to 21st-century American individuals."[43]

In an article in a 1996 issue of the Adventist Review, Calvin Rock quoted this question:

"I am a longtime church elder and highly supportive of the denomination. But in my opinion the General Conference erred when it ruled favorably on wedding rings. Now not only do we have sparkling rings of all kinds in our church, but also, we have other jewelry, most notably earrings. Are earrings now acceptable? If not, what can be done?"[44]

In his answer, Rock quoted point 2 from the 1972 Annual Council action (quoted on page 26 of this booklet) and then referred to the 1986 NAD action. He reasserted the idea that "plain wedding rings" are "nonjewelry," but then stated:

"However, neither action [1972 or 1986] 'rules favorably' on wedding rings. In fact, the NAD action questions the need for their use in its territory, since they are not, as in many parts of the world, deemed obligatory.

"Further caution is provided in the NAD statement that ministers are counseled not to perform ring ceremonies, since the wearing of the wedding band still 'is not regarded as ... an imperative custom in North America.'

"What is unfortunate is that some individuals have abused the option these rulings provide by wearing extravagant wedding rings and other jewelry, including earrings. These individuals go to extremes (some, no doubt, unknowingly) and are in clear violation of both the General Conference and North American Division position."[45]

Having now surveyed the history of the development of the use of the wedding ring, I wish to state several reasons why I believe Seventh-day Adventists should reject and abandon this cultural practice and why I think believers should place their influence in this direction.

---

[1] Ellen G. White, *Life Sketches*, p. 196.

[2] "We are told in various ways by Eusebius, that Constantine, in order to recommend the new religion to the heathen, transferred into it the outward ornaments to which they had been accustomed in their own ... [H]oly water; ... the ring in marriage, turning to the East, images ... are all of pagan origin, and sanctified by their adoption into the Church." J.H. Newman, An Essay on the Development of Christian Doctrine, pp. 359 360. Newman was a cardinal in the Roman Catholic Church in the 19th century.

[3] Alexander Rogers and Alice Beard, *Five Thousand Years of Gems and Jewelry*, pp. 37-39 quoted in "The Wedding Ring Concept in the SDA Church," p. 4, a term paper (1985) by Eliezer Castanon found in the Heritage Room of the library at Andrews University. The practice of wearing a wedding ring actually grew out of the betrothal (engagement) ring. The man or his family gave the girl or her family a betrothal ring as a symbol of a piece of money. It was given as "earnest money," not unlike the dowry (James Remington McCarthy, *Rings Through the Ages*, p. 161). Later it took on the additional meaning that the woman was "already taken." It was not until much later that the addition of the wedding ring occurred, apparently about the time of the Protestant Reformation (McCarthy, p. 156, 157). At first, the betrothal ring, after being given at the time of engagement, was taken back and given to the woman again at the time of the wedding ceremony. Later, a separate ring was given at the time of the marriage ceremony.

[4] Cf. *Genesis 41:42; Esther 3:10; 8:2*, etc.

[5] See *Genesis 24:22, 47, 53*.

[6] See *Exodus 12:35-36*.

[7] *Exodus 35:5, 22.*

[8] As in *Ezekiel 16:9-13*.

[9] As in *Luke 15:22*.

[10] As in *Isaiah 61:10*.

[11] *Ezekiel 16:9-13*.

[12] *Revelation 17:3-4*.

[13] Indeed, this has been true throughout history. Reformationists such as Presbyterians and Anabaptists of the 16h century, the Puritan reforms a

century later, the Wesleyan and Whitefield revivals of the 18th century, and the Great Second Advent Awakening of the 19th century, all emphasized such reform, including not wearing the wedding ring.

[14] *Genesis 35:1-2, 4.*

[15] *Exodus 33:5-6.*

[16] *1 Timothy 2:9-10.*

[17] *1 Peter 3:3-5.*

[18] Ellen G. White, *Testimonies for the Church*, Vol. 4, pp. 644, 645.

[19] Ibid., pp. 647-648.

[20] In the section on "The form of solemnization of Matrimonie," the 1637 edition of *The Book of Common Prayer*, and *Administration of the Sacraments*, indicates that the wedding ring continued to be used in the Anglican Church.

[21] "The Wedding Ring Concept in the SDA Church," pp. 11-12, a term paper (1985) by Eliezer Castanon found in the Heritage Room of the library at Andrews University. See also Charles Colcock Jones, Tracts on Doctrine, Tract 174, "The Glory of Woman," Vol. 9, p. 6. *The Manual of Presbyterian Law and Usage* (1873) for the first time permitted ministers, if the couple to be married desired it, to use a ring in the marriage ceremony.

[22] That a wedding ring was not typically used by Baptists is revealed in comments made by Francis Wayland in *Notes on the Principles and Practices of Baptist Churches* (1857), "Marriage and Funeral Services," p. 163.

[23] For instance, see "Of the Celebration of Matrimony," *The Practical Works of Richard Baxter*, pp. 937-938, where the form of the marriage service consisted of the couple clasping hands and did not include the use of a wedding ring. Richard Baxter lived from 1615 to 1691.

[24] That Methodists did not permit jewelry, including the wedding ring, is seen from a statement of principles and doctrines approved in 1784 and published in 1791. That publication includes this catechical passage:"Quest. Should we insist on the rules concerning dress?

"Answ. By all means. This is no time to give any encouragement to superfluity of apparel. Therefore give no ticket to any, till they have left off superfluous ornaments. In order to this, 1. Let every Deacon read the thoughts upon dress, at least once a year in every large society.   2. In visiting the classes, be very mild, but very strict. 3. Allow of no exempt case, not even of a married woman: Better one suffer than many.   4. Give no tickets to any that wear high heads, enormous bonnets, ruffles, or rings." ("Tickets" were required to participate in communion, a sign of membership and good standing.) Not until the Doctrines and Discipline statement

of 1872, some 88 years later, did the Methodists permit the
ring to be used in a marriage ceremony.

[25] A good example of this is John Wesley's sermon "On Dress," in which
he expounds on *1 Peter 3:3-4*. *Wesley's Works*, Vol. VII, pp. 15-26 (1872
edition).

[26] D.T. Bourdeau, "Wearing of Gold," *Advent Review and Sabbath Herald*,
October 5, 1869, Vol. 34, p. 117.

[27] Ellen G. White, "Extravagance in Dress," *Second Advent Review and
Sabbath Herald*, July 8, 1880.

[28] Ibid., March 28, 1882.

[29] Ibid., *Testimonies to Ministers and Gospel Workers*, p. 181. Her full
statement will be dealt with at greater length below.

[30] It should be noted that all during the centuries since the custom of
the wedding ring began, it applied only to women. "The wedding ring
was an extension of the engagement ring. In the Roman culture, the
man who was interested in a woman would go out and purchase a ring.
... [H]e would give it to his promised one, indicating to the public that
this woman was not 'for sale.' It was a sort of commercial pledge, that
the contract would be completed." ("The Wedding Ring Concept in the
SDA Church," p. 4, a term paper (1985) by Eliezer Castanon found in
the Heritage Room of the library at Andrews University.) However, during the Second World War, there was a move by wives of soldiers to
have them also wear a wedding ring. (James Remington McCarthy,
Rings Through the Ages, p. 182.) Apparently they were concerned about
their husbands' temptations as they called at various ports and felt that
if the wives were required to be chaste and wear a ring as a symbol of
that, then their husbands should have the same requirement. So the
"double ring ceremony" was born, in which both bride and groom
received a wedding ring. However, the custom of only the woman wearing an engagement ring has prevailed.

[31] *Minutes of the Officers Meeting of the General Conference*, October 2,
1972, p. 3 (72 411).

[32] "Recommendations of General Interest From the Autumn Council
1972—1," *Review and Herald*, November 30, 1972, p. 16. This is the
statement as it appeared in the *Review* under the heading "Display and
Adornment."

[33] Roland Churchman, *Spectrum*: 1974, Vol. 6, Nos. 1, 2, pp. 74-75.

[34] Ibid., p. 74 (author's emphasis).

[35] Carl G. Tuland, "Let's Stop Arguing Over the Wedding Ring,"
Spectrum: 1977, Vol. 8, No. 2, pp. 59-61 (author's emphasis).

[36] "Jewelry—a Clarification and Appeal," *Adventist Review*, August 4,
1988, p. 15.

[37] Joe Crews, "A Response to the General Conference Action of October,

1986 Concerning the Wedding Ring."

[38] Calvin B. Rock, "The Wedding Ring," *Adventist Review*, August 4, 1988, p. 14.

[39] Roger W. Coon, "Reviving Ancient Paganism?" *Adventist Review*, June 11, 1987, p. 10.

[40] Ibid., Calvin B. Rock, p. 15.

[41] Joe Crews, op. cit.

[42] Ibid.

[43] Williams, op. cit.

[44] Calvin B. Rock, "Gems and Jewels," *Adventist Review*, October 24, 1996, p. 29.

[45] Ibid.

Is It OK Because It's Cultural?

"This is the crux of the matter, for wearing a wedding band is not a question of morals or sin; it is merely one of the customs, which vary with national and social concepts."
—Carl G. Tuland[1]

"All that we urge is compliance with the injunctions of God's word. Are we Bible readers and followers of Bible teachings? Will we obey God, or conform to the customs of the world? Will we serve God or mammon? Can we expect to enjoy peace of mind and the approval of God while walking directly contrary to the teachings of His word?"
—Ellen White[2]

I understand Tuland's argument to be that wearing a wedding band is not a moral issue but simply a cultural one, and therefore it is okay to wear a ring. If that is true, then the opposite is also true. If it is not a moral issue, then it is also okay not to wear a ring, and when a church or organization asks it members not to wear one it is not violating any moral code.

To pursue one cultural point further, here's something I find really curious. People in the late

20th and early 21st centuries, including some within our own church, have become very concerned about not transporting our "Western Christianity" to other countries where we undertake missionary activity, lest we confuse "Westernism" with Christianity. But isn't it curious that Adventist missionaries who have adopted the wedding ring usually take it with them wherever they go? Previously, most of the cultures to which they have traveled did not have this practice in their culture. Indeed, they may have had a different cultural way of indicating marriage. And yet, this Western practice has been introduced (and continues to be introduced) into cultures where it previously had no meaning and had not been practiced. In some cases, this involved requiring new converts to remove their jewelry, including finger rings, but then teaching them to wear a wedding ring because of its significance in Western cultures. This is blatant cultural imperialism, which should be abandoned.

---

[1] Op. cit.

[2] Ellen G. White, *Testimonies for the Church*, Vol. 4, p. 644.

It's Not OK Just Because It's Cultural

As indicated before, the engagement ring apparently arose first and was only much later followed by the use of a wedding ring. Rings have been worn throughout history for various reasons and to mean various things. Other cultures have practices to indicate marriage in other ways—some of them involving other forms of jewelry.

For late 20th-century Adventists to try to single out the wearing of the wedding ring as an acceptable cultural practice is really untenable if one wishes to take Scripture and divinely inspired counsel seriously.

There is no Biblical warrant for adopting cultural practices that vary from Biblical principles just because a culture has attached some particular significance to it. If so, then we would need to allow for all kinds of unbiblical practices around the world based on this rationale. Further, there is no sound logical basis for adopting the wedding ring and not the engagement ring, since they mean essentially the same thing. And still further, if you allow for wedding and engagement rings, there is no logical basis for disallowing other types of jewelry that have significant cultural and personal meaning, such as friendship rings, class rings, Superbowl rings, etc. In the final analysis, if you allow certain types of jewelry because of cultural significance, you must logically allow for most any jewelry because the culture or person attaches some sort of significance to it.

Are we really prepared to crown culture "king" and have it supplant clear statements of Scripture? If we do this, do we not fall under Jesus' condemnation when He said, *"For laying aside the commandment of God, you hold the tradition of men ... all too well you reject the commandment of God, that you may keep your tradition."*[1] All these difficulties are avoided if we will simply remain true to Scripture and the inspired counsel given through Ellen White.

In the end, it really does come down to the questions inspiration has posed: "All that we urge is compliance with the injunctions of God's word. Are we Bible readers and followers of Bible teachings? Will we obey God, or conform to the customs of the world?"[2]

---

[1] *Mark 7:8-9.*
[2] Ibid., Ellen G. White.

The Wedding Ring *Is* Jewelry

The rationale that has been used to justify the adoption of the wedding ring is that it is not jewelry. If by this it is meant that the wedding ring is not jewelry just like any other costume jewelry, the point can be granted. It is not like earrings, a bracelet, or a necklace, which are for ornamentation only. It is jewelry to which special significance has been attached, signifying marriage. It is jewelry nonetheless.

The argument that it is not jewelry is a more modern innovation. Such a distinction was not made by early Christians before the adoption of the practice, nor was it made by the churches of the Reformation and movements of subsequent centuries, which rejected jewelry. The wedding ring was considered jewelry, and as such it was rejected as a violation of the Biblical injunction not to "wear gold."

It would appear that this modern invention is an argument of convenience by those who have wanted to adopt the custom and yet feel like they were not coming under the condemnation of Scripture against the wearing of jewelry. However, this is a transparent argument that will not bear the scrutiny of history or reason.

The engagement ring has essentially the same significance as the wedding ring. Yet the current official position of the church in North

America is to disallow the engagement ring, and many North American Division Seventh-day Adventists who favor the wedding ring forego the engagement ring. On what basis? Because it is jewelry and the wedding ring isn't? Obviously not. Can such a distinction be defended from the Bible, the Spirit of Prophecy, or reason? The answer is obvious, and this illogical distinction is already beginning to break down in North America, where quite a number of young Adventist couples are beginning to adopt the practice of exchanging engagement rings as well as wedding rings.

The attempt to redefine a reality as a non-reality helps nothing. It is merely engaging in self-deception.

Secular society is not so burdened to say that a wedding ring is not jewelry. A number of years ago, I watched a program on public television about a family who was struggling to make a living in the gold fields of Australia in the latter 1800s. To try to make ends meet, they sold whatever they felt they could do without. Finally, in desperation, the husband and wife talked of pawning their wedding rings. The husband objected, but the wife reasoned, "You love me, and I love you, and we don't need jewelry to prove it." So they pawned their wedding rings. I found it instructive that the Australian and British scriptwriters included this dialogue in the film. They obviously had no problem identifying a wedding ring as jewelry.

It Puts the EmPHAsis
on the Wrong SylLABle

P art of the problem with following the wedding ring custom is that it tends to teach that by putting something on the external, it will keep the internal (in me and in the other person) clean and moral. Actually, the opposite is true. Only a moral, clean, and committed "internal" keeps the external behaviors clean and moral.

This is clearly the teaching of Scripture, such as when Jesus and His disciples were criticized for not engaging in the ceremonial washing of hands before eating. Jesus said, *"Not what goes into the mouth defiles a man; but what comes out of the mouth, this defiles a man ... those things which proceed out of the mouth come from the heart, and they defile a man. For out of the heart proceed evil thoughts, murders, adulteries, fornications, thefts, false witness, blasphemies."*[1]

Many say they wear a wedding ring as a symbol of purity and commitment. If this is the case, then something is terribly wrong. In the last 100 years virtually all Protestant churches have dropped their opposition to the wedding ring, and members have adopted the custom. Yet affairs, adultery, and divorce have multiplied. Inspiration says the wearing of a wedding ring is no evidence that the wearers are true to their marriage vows.[2] How many men and women flirt and even commit adultery while they are wearing a wedding ring? We are all painfully aware of this reality.

Ultimately, just as Jesus said, it's not what's on the outside that makes the difference; it's what's on the inside. For Christians and last-day Seventh-day Adventists, that's where the emphasis should lie. As the apostles Peter and Paul counseled, let's emphasize an adorning of the character with the qualities of Christ.

---

[1] Certainly, ministers and other gospel workers who study with people prior to baptism should deal sensitively and gently with persons on this point. The first paragraph of point 3 in the 1972 statement is appropriate counsel in this regard. Typically, ministers who follow this counsel have said they have no real problems with new converts on the matter.

[2] See 1972, 1986, and 1996 statements above.

[3] *Matthew 15:11, 18-19.*

[4] Ellen G. White, *Testimonies to Ministers and Gospel Workers*, p. 181.

It Places Our Feet on the Slippery Slope

*"You will say that these are very small sins;
and doubtless, like all young tempters, you
are anxious to be able to report spectacular
wickedness. But do remember, the only
thing that matters is the extent to which
you separate the man from the Enemy. It
does not matter how small the sins are,
provided that their cumulative effect is to
edge the man away from the Light and out
into the Nothing. Murder is no better than
cards if cards can do the trick. Indeed, the
safest road to Hell is the gradual one—the
gentle slope, soft underfoot, without sud-
den turnings, without milestones, without
signposts."*[1]

—Screwtape Letters

So says the senior tempter, Screwtape, to his
underling, Wormwood, in the classic book
Screwtape Letters. This passage states what I
believe to be one of the main problems with the
adoption of the wedding ring. It places our feet
on that "gentle slope," which gradually leads to
increasing compromise.

As our historical survey revealed, the
Seventh-day Adventist Church has not been the
only church to ask its members not to wear a
wedding ring. At one time this was the position

of the Methodists, the Presbyterians, the Baptists, and others. Their rationale for doing so was the same as that which led the Adventist Church to take this position—the Bible's teaching regarding doing away with outward adornment. However, in time these churches began to drop their opposition to the wedding ring, and the result is plain for all to see. They went on to condone jewelry in all its forms.

Since the Adventist Church in North America modified its stance toward allowing members to follow the wedding ring custom, that decision has been followed by the adoption of costume jewelry by a good number of members in the church. Moreover, in countries where Adventists have historically worn the wedding ring, the adoption of all kinds of costume jewelry is, in general, even further in advance of the church in North America.

Without exception, every church or group who formerly opposed use of the wedding ring and then afterward dropped its objection went on to adopt all forms of jewelry. We should be asking ourselves if that is where we want to go. Is that the direction toward which we want to lend our influence? When the very same change is currently happening in our own church, believers who take the Word of God and the counsels of the Spirit of Prophecy seriously should be asking themselves if that is where they want our church to end up. Is this the end toward which you want to cast your influence?

Members may wish to rationalize by saying the wedding ring is not jewelry, but when they go on to openly condone costume jewelry in all forms, they cannot do so without clearly falling outside the pale of being faithful to Biblical teaching.

Many may believe we can adopt the wedding ring and have it stop there. This is a fallacy. To drop opposition to the wearing of the wedding ring is not to end the battle; it only changes the battle lines. The argument is for a "simple, unadorned wedding band." Realistically, though, how many pastors or church members are going to tell the baptismal candidate who is wearing a diamond wedding ring that she must replace it with "a simple, unadorned wedding band" before she can be baptized? It won't happen. So, the unrealistic hope of "simple, unadorned" goes out the window. Thus the battle line moves again. It moves to the engagement ring. This battle line is breaking down, so the battle line is next moved to various forms of costume jewelry. Trying to make logical and Biblical distinctions in these various places cannot be done, and it is a slippery slope indeed.

Early Adventist Daniel T. Bourdeau, quoted earlier when he decried the adoption of jewelry by other denominations, went on to write the following as to why Adventist members should not "wear gold:"

"It sets a bad example, and hinders a good reform. Like begets like. If the weak, who love show, see us wear gold to a small degree, they think they are justified in putting it on to a greater extent. For, say they, gold is gold, and such a brother or sister wears it, and I can."[2]

The concern over negative influence was likewise voiced by Ellen White in her 1880 statement. "That ring encircling your finger may be very plain, but it is useless, and the wearing of it has a wrong influence upon others."[3] She was also concerned about the slippery-slope effect. Her 1882 article entitled "Where Are We Drifting?" showed her concern about compromise. In her major 1892 statement she said, "I feel deeply over this leavening process which seems to be going on among us, in the conformity to custom and fashion."[4] Elsewhere she wrote, "Obedience to fashion is pervading our Seventh-day Adventist churches and is doing more than any other power to separate our people from God ... There is a terrible sin upon us as a people, that we have permitted our church members to dress in a manner inconsistent with their faith. We must arise at once and close the door against the allurements of fashion. Unless we do this, our churches will become demoralized."[5]

Each believer must decide in which direction to cast his or her influence. The best and safest course to pursue is not to put our foot on that slippery slope in the first place, but to remain faithful to the divine counsel we have, regardless of what popular society says.

[1] C.S. Lewis, *Screwtape Letters*, p. 54, First Touchstone Edition 1996.

[2] Daniel T. Bourdeau, "Wearing of Gold," *Advent Review and Sabbath Herald*, October 5, 1869, Vol. 34, p. 117.

[3] Ellen G. White, *Testimonies for the Church*, Vol. 4, p. 630

[4] Ibid., *Testimonies to Ministers and Gospel Workers*, p. 181.

[5] Ibid., *Testimonies for the Church*, Vol. 4, pp. 647-648.

Ellen White's
Major Statement Considered

I would like to quote in its entirety Ellen White's major statement on the wedding ring, written in a letter dated Aug. 2, 1892:

"Some have had a burden in regard to the wearing of a marriage ring, feeling that the wives of our ministers should conform to this custom. All this is unnecessary. Let the ministers' wives have the golden link which binds their souls to Jesus Christ, a pure and holy character, the true love and meekness and godliness that are the fruit borne upon the Christian tree, and their influence will be secure anywhere. The fact that a disregard of the custom occasions remark is no good reason for adopting it. Americans can make their position understood by plainly stating that the custom is not regarded as obligatory in our country. We need not wear the sign, for we are not untrue to our vow, and the wearing of the ring would be no evidence that we were true. I feel deeply over this leavening process which seems to be going on among us, in the conformity to custom and fashion. Not one penny should be spent for a circlet of gold to testify that we are married. In countries where the custom is imperative, we have no burden to condemn those who have their marriage ring; let them wear it if they can do so conscientiously; but let not our missionaries feel that the wearing of the ring will increase their influence one jot or tittle. If they are Christians, it will be manifest in their Christlikeness of character, in their words, in their works, in the home, in association with others; it will be evinced by their patience and long suffering and kindliness. They will manifest the spirit of the Master, they will possess His beauty of character, His loveliness of disposition, His sympathetic heart."[1]

First, I would like to pose a "bottom line" kind of question. Does an objective reading of this statement urge the reader toward adopting the use of a wedding ring or away from the practice? I believe it is evident that the burden of the statement, and indeed of all of Ellen White's counsel relating to the topic, is not to find a way to adopt the practice and feel justified in doing so, but rather to discourage the practice in the face of all circumstances.

Let's take a look at the main points in her statement:

"All This Is Unnecessary"

The reasons she gives as to why the wearing of a wedding ring is unnecessary could be summarized like this:

1. A Christlike, pure character is what really protects Christians and their influence anywhere.
2. Christians need not wear a ring because they are not untrue to their marriage vow.
3. A ring is no evidence that the person wearing it is true to the marriage vow.
4. Wearing the ring does not increase a person's influence for good.
5. Christian character is what gives the person influence for good.

Not a Reason For Adopting

"The fact that a disregard of the custom occasions remark is no good reason for adopting it." Questions and comments by others is one of the main reasons urged by those who wear or want to wear the wedding ring. Yet the inspired counsel clearly is that this is not a good reason for wearing a wedding ring.

Leavening Process

"I feel deeply over this leavening process which seems to be going on among us, in the conformity to custom and fashion." I have already referred to this above, but we should notice that Ellen White regarded the move toward conformity to this custom as a deleterious compromise, a leavening of God's church and people that was to be decried and shunned.

Not One Penny for a Ring

"Not one penny should be spent for a circlet of gold to testify that we are married." Here she invokes the Biblical principle of good stewardship. God's people should not expend even one penny of their resources to follow this unnecessary custom. Do a little math with me. We will only "ballpark it," but this will help make the point. There are now approximately 11 million baptized Seventh-day Adventist members around the world. How many of those are married? I don't know, but let's approach it in a way that will yield a conservative estimate. In the United States, there are about three persons per household. If, because of larger families in some other countries, we were to figure an average of six persons per household worldwide, two of whom are married adults, this would yield more than 3 million married adult Adventist members. If they all wore a wedding

ring costing an average of U.S. $40 (some pay a whole lot more than that), this would add up to a total investment of nearly $150 million in wedding rings. If an average of 10 percent of the children of those adult members married each year (10 percent of more than 7 million), this would add nearly $30 million worth of wedding rings every year. When you consider that many rings would be purchased for subsequent marriages, you have only begun. Engagement rings are also being adopted, and have you ever seen a $40 engagement ring? The stewardship issue is not insignificant.

Accommodation

But what about Ellen White's statement that says it's okay in areas where it's widely practiced? Well, let's take a good look at her accommodating statement:

> "In countries where the custom is imperative, we have no burden to condemn those who have their marriage ring; let them wear it if they can do so conscientiously ..."

Let's notice three points and then try to answer the following question: If the practice is really wrong, why did God's inspired messenger make an allowance such as this?

1. <u>Where custom is imperative.</u> She applies her counsel to members living in "*countries where the custom is imperative.*" What constitutes imperative? Is it the percentage of the population that follows the practice? I think not, since the percentage of American women following the practice in Ellen White's day was perhaps not greatly different from the percentage in Australia or Europe. Only U.S. Seventh-day Adventists (plus those in a number of mission fields) and a few other small church groups abstained from the practice by the time she wrote this statement. Obviously it is not defined, but I believe it had more to do with attitudes and beliefs than numbers.

Probably most Adventists who argue in favor of Americans adopting the wedding ring believe that whatever constituted "imperative" in 1892 now applies to North America. To the contrary, I would suggest that the opposite is true. The percentages (other than adding some men at the time of WWII) have probably not changed that much in the last 100 years. And rather than the beliefs and attitudes around the world being more "imperative" now than in 1892, they are clearly less imperative. Pluralism and tolerance has rendered

much freer circumstances most anywhere in the world. One Seventh-day
Adventist pastor, native to a northern
European country, did not wear a wedding ring in his country nor did his
wife. He told me they got no "flak" from
anyone except Adventist Church members. Is that instructive?

2. <u>No burden to condemn.</u> She said that
"we have no burden to condemn" those in
such countries who wore a wedding
ring. No burden to condemn is very different than urging the practice. The
writer of the 1974 Spectrum article
inadvertently had it right when he said
Ellen White's position was to "tolerate
its use."

3. <u>A matter of conscience.</u> She wrote: *"let
them wear it if they can do so conscientiously."* Where conscience is involved,
moral dimensions are involved, not just
cultural ones. The church was correct in
its 1972 action when it called upon ministers and gospel workers to "[P]ress the
claims of the gospel upon the conscience of the candidates, encouraging
careful self-examination concerning the
motives involved in decisions that must
be made." Ellen White's 1892 statement
would make this counsel appropriate

for ministers and gospel workers around the world. Her statement suggests the possibility that if members in the countries to which she was referring would do this, they might decide not to follow the practice, for conscience' sake.

So why did Ellen White provide counsel with this statement? It is clearly a statement of accommodation—an exception, rather than indicating the direction God would have the entire church go. The trajectory of her counsel is away from the practice, not toward the practice, as some would have us believe.

But why allow an exception? There are Biblical precedents for this. While I am not suggesting that the gravity of the two matters are parallel, but only that the exception principle is the same, I would point you to the matter of divorce and remarriage. In Moses' time he permitted rather "easy divorce." A man simply had to write out a certificate of divorce, hand it to his wife, and send her on her way.[2] Centuries later Jesus, in commenting on this, did not condemn Moses for permitting it, but said, *"From the beginning it was not so. And I say to you, whoever divorces his wife, except for sexual immorality, and marries another, commits adultery; and whoever marries her who is divorced commits adultery."*[3] Jesus called God's people to a higher standard, a reform back toward God's original plan.

I would suggest this is the model for what we see in this case with the wedding ring accommodation. The exception is not the rule; it is an exception. God's will is in a different direction. The Bible and the inspired counsels through Ellen White clearly indicate that God is calling His people to a higher standard.

---

[1] Ibid., *Testimonies to Ministers*, pp. 180-181.

[2] *Deuteronomy 24:1.*

[3] *Matthew 19:8-9.*

Let Us Be Faithful in This Small Thing, Else How Shall We Fair in Larger Things?

Some are saying this is an insignificant issue with which the church should not concern itself. Consider again the words of Screwtape to the novice tempter, Wormword. "Murder is no better than cards if cards can do the trick."[1]

Yes, in the entire scheme of things, this is a small thing.[2] Yet remember this: It is important enough for God to address it.

It's important, but it's not the whole picture. I believe God looks at the larger picture, at the tendencies and trends. So what are some of the larger implications?

Nineteenth-century Anglican bishop J.C. Ryle, writing on a different topic, makes a very pertinent point for our case:

> "The things I have spoken of are trifles, I fully concede. But they are pernicious trifles, because they are the outward expression of an inward doctrine. They are the skin disease which is the symptom of an unsound constitution. They are the plague spot which tells of internal poison. They are the curling smoke which arises from a hidden volcano of mischief."[3]

While the inspired counsel tolerates the wearing of a wedding ring in countries where it is considered obligatory, if those members can do so in good conscience, the larger picture is that the practice is rather to be avoided. Wearing the wedding band tends to encourage the wearing of all kinds of jewelry, which clearly comes under the disapproval of Bible teaching. If members go on to adopt jewelry in all of its various forms, contrary to clear Bible teaching (which is happening), this bodes ill for remaining faithful to God and His word in larger matters when public and societal pressure is on.[4] If we are willing to compromise and vary from clear Bible teaching in the smaller matter of adornment and jewelry, where the worst that can happen is "discomfort" and "embarrassment,"[5] will we also be willing to compromise on bigger things when our livelihood and perhaps life itself is at stake? It is the small victories that help prepare us for the larger ones. If we fail in the smaller ones, it is much more likely that we will fail in the larger ones. "If you have run with the footmen, and they have wearied you, Then how can you contend with horses? And if in the land of peace, In which you trusted, they wearied you, Then how will you do in the floodplain of the Jordan?"[6]

God is calling out a remnant, as indicated in the book of *Revelation.* The main characteristic of that remnant is that they *"hold to the word of God and the testimony of Jesus."* This point is repeated in various ways throughout the book at least eight times.[7] It says, *"they did not love their lives to the death."*[8] Indeed, this is true since *Revelation* tells us that *"I saw under the altar the souls of those who had been slain for the word of God and for the testimony which they held."*[9] It is these whom *Revelation* reveals as the final victors with Christ.[10]

We are living in the last days. We have said to God, "Yes, we choose to be among the remnant who hold to Your Word." Now is no time to quiver and quail in the face of social and peer pressure. We will have much more difficult things to face in the not-too-distant future. "The important future is before us. To meet its trials and temptations, and to perform its duties, will require great faith, energy, and perseverance."[11] "We need to stay our faith upon God, for there is just before us a time that will try men's souls."[12]

Remember, "All that we urge is compliance with the injunctions of God's word. ... [I]t is God who condescends to give us these instructions; they are the declarations of Infinite Wisdom, and those who disregard them do so at their own peril and loss."[13]

---

[1] C.S. Lewis, op. cit.

[2] While this may be regarded as a small thing, the Biblical injunction against the wearing of jewelry is just as plainly taught in Scripture, and perhaps more so, than is baptism by immersion.

[3] J.C. Ryle, *Light From Old Times*, p. 47 (emphasis in the original).

[4] What will be our position on issues such as homosexual practice, various forms of popular entertainment, social drinking of alcohol, evolu-

tion as the explanation of origins, and many others for which there is strong societal pressure to conform?

5 See the "Roland Churchman" article in *Spectrum.*

6 *Jeremiah 12:5.*

7 See the following: *Revelation 1:2, 9; 6:9; 12:11, 17; 19:10, 13; 20:4.*

8 *Revelation 12:11.*

9 *Revelation 6:9* (emphasis supplied).

10 *Revelation 20:4.*

11 Ellen G. White, *Advent Review and Sabbath Herald*, Jan. 11, 1887, p. 18.

12 Ibid., *Testimonies for the Church,* Vol. 5, p. 753.

13 Ellen G. White, *Testimonies for the Church,* Vol. 4, p. 644.

Summary and Appeal

'Cause when we say no to the things of the world
We open our hearts to the love of the Lord
And it's hard to imagine the freedom we find
From the things we leave behind.
                                    —Michael Card[1]

Throughout history God has communicated through inspired writers that He wishes His people to be characterized by simplicity. He has asked them to adorn their characters, not their bodies. The wedding ring came into the Christian church from pagan nations and practices in the centuries after Christ. Throughout history, revivals and reforms have typically included abandoning outward adornment and jewelry. Following the adoption of the wedding ring by the Christian church, subsequent revivals and reforms also typically included abandoning the wedding ring custom since it was understood to violate the Bible call not to "wear gold."

As churches that formerly taught their members not to follow the wedding ring custom dropped their opposition, they all, without exception, went on to adopt costume jewelry in all forms.[2] The same trends can be seen currently in the Seventh-day Adventist Church.

Official church decisions have sought to

accommodate members who have wanted to adopt the custom while still discouraging the practice and calling on leaders and church workers to "press the claims of the gospel" and fully present the teachings of the Spirit of Prophecy to members. By in large, this is not being done because "no minister is comfortable in taking arbitrary positions based on church rules rather than God's rules."

As members of the remnant, we each are faced with deciding in which direction to cast our influence. Will it be with custom and tradition, even if it violates the principles of the word of God, or will it be with the "word of God and the testimony of Jesus" even if this varies from common custom? While the wearing of a wedding ring may be regarded as a trifle, it is a trifle with much larger implications.

> The remnant of God will face much larger issues in the near future with much more serious consequences. How will we fare in much more significant matters then, if we stumble on small things now?

---

[1] "Things We Leave Behind," by Michael Card, Scott Roley, and Phil Madeira, Mole End Music (1982).

[2] Most have gone on to adopt other practices, due to societal pressures, which are clear violations of Bible teachings such as defending homosexual practices and ordaining practicing homosexuals as "ministers of the gospel."

Appeal to Ministers and Their Families

Your responsibilities as remnant Christians are even more extensive because of your role in the church. Church members look to you as the example and bastion of the church in faithfully preaching the gospel and Adventist message and living it out. You should definitely be the "head and not the tail" in this matter of adornment and the wedding ring. If you adopt this custom you cast your influence in the opposite direction from that laid down in Scripture and the counsels of the Spirit of Prophecy.

I appeal with all my heart and soul for you not to do that. Let us be faithful to God and His word. Let's graciously, but clearly, cast our influence in this direction. I appeal to church leaders to lead in this stance. I appeal to all church workers to follow and support this stance with your whole life and influence. I appeal to the spouses of church workers to join in supporting and following this stance of faithfulness.

Therefore we also, since we are surrounded by so great a cloud of witnesses, let us lay aside every weight, and the sin which so easily ensnares us, and let us run with endurance the race that is set before us, looking unto Jesus, the author and finisher of our faith, who for the joy that was set before Him endured the cross, despising the shame, and has sat down at the right hand of the throne of God. For consider Him who endured such hostility from sinners against Himself, lest you become weary and discouraged in your souls (*Hebrews 12:1-3*).